GLEANINGS
AND GIFTINGS

Also by H. D. Wagener

The Entire Packet: Poems on Physical and Spiritual Reality; iUniverse, 175 p.; www.amazon.com/books.

Intimations of the Soul of a Seeker, iUniverse, 54 p. The poems in this book comprise Part 1 of *Gleanings and Giftings.*

The Web site www.hdpoetry.com contains poems, comments on H. D.'s poetry, direct links to the books on Amazon.com/books, thoughts on meditation, and practices in meditation.

The Granitic Stone Resources of South Carolina; South Carolina Geological Survey, Mineral Resources Series 5, 65 p., 24 maps appended.
Petrology of the Granites, Adamellites and Related Metamorphic Rocks of the Winnsboro 15' Quadrangle, South Carolina; The Citadel Monograph Series, Number X, 75 p.
Uranium Resource Evaluation, Portland Quadrangle, Maine and New Hampshire; U. S. Department of Energy, Grand Junction, CO, 110 p.
Petrology of the Wilson Creek Gneiss; Western North Carolina, and Its Relation to the Grandfather Mountain Formation; Chiasma Consultants, Inc., 57 p.
Uranium Mineralization in the Wilson Creek and Cranberry Gneisses and the Grandfather Mountain Formation, North Carolina and Tennessee; J. G. McHone, coauthor; U.S. Department of Energy, Open File Report PGJ-076, 35 p.
National Uranium Resource Evaluation: Glens Falls Quadrangle, New York - Vermont - New Hampshire: J. G. McHone, coauthor; U.S. Department of Energy, Open File Report PGJ-025, 39 p.

GLEANINGS
AND GIFTINGS

POEMS BY
H. D. WAGENER

iUniverse, Inc.
New York   Bloomington

GLEANINGS AND GIFTINGS

iUniverse books may be ordered through booksellers or by contacting:

iUniverse
1663 Liberty Drive
Bloomington, IN 47403
www.iuniverse.com
1-800-Authors (1-800-288-4677)

ISBN: 978-1-4401-5023-4 (pbk)
ISBN: 978-1-4401-5024-1 (ebk)

Library of Congress Control Number: 2009930717

Printed in the United States of America
iUniverse rev. date: 7/17/2009

Dedicated to Sri Eknath Easwaran, a mini-mystic by his own definition, and H. D.'s principal teacher in the second half of life.

Contents

Introduction

H. D. Wagener has written poems on physical and spiritual reality for twenty-nine years. During most of that time, he became thoroughly conversant with the earth and cosmos as a researcher/teacher, meditated, and studied mystical literature under an Indian Hindu teacher who emphasized Hindu, Christian, and Buddhist texts. For twenty years, he worked at carpentry and whatever came to hand in an unsuccessful attempt to support a family in semi-bourgeois style in Maine. He has taught courses on the meditative life and the Perennial Philosophy in the Osher Lifelong Learning Institute at the University of Southern Maine. A Virginian, H. D. emigrated to New England with his second wife Judy Plano and four children in 1978. He lives in Portland, Maine, with his third wife, Marion Lundgren, a Nova Scotian. His children are scattered from Maine to New York to California.

H. D.'s first book of 100 poems, *The Entire Packet: Poems on Physical and Spiritual Reality,* was published in 2004 and was followed by another, *Intimations of the Soul of a Seeker,* in 2006. The body of poems in *Intimations* was incorporated into *Gleanings and Giftings* as its first section (Part 1). One poem in this group has been revised. "Mind Power" has been given a subtitle, and several new lines have been added at the end. Part 2 of *Gleanings and Giftings* consists of twenty-six new poems written from May 2006 through October 2008.

Some of the poems offered in *Gleanings and Giftings* are attempts to walk the limn separating the unreal from the real—all that is impermanent from That Which Is. This limn is a boundary drawn by the mind, whose surface H. D. has occasionally observed internally (see definition at Notes, Definitions). H. D. accepts that the limn cannot be crossed intellectually. He has attempted to walk the limn to test the limits of the intellect, and, perhaps, to attract the Light, the grace that wells up from within, without which the limn remains impenetrable.

During the writing of the twenty-six new poems, H. D. realized that he had been released from the need to attempt intellectual expression of approaches to that which lies beyond the limn. He waited six or eight months until it was confirmed internally that this was so. H. D. is done for now with this topic as a writer, but not with hovering about the limn. Publication of *Gleanings and Giftings* marks a turning point for H. D., one which, at this point, has not been fathomed. What will emerge from here on remains to be seen.

If any of these poems should induce you to begin your own long-postponed investigation of the limn, H. D. would smile deeply, but he recommends that you first seek grace. Why beat around the bush? Check out the *Meditation* page on http://www. hdpoetry.com.

Part 1
Poems from January 2004
through April 2006

The Apostles' Creed

Between Mary and Pilate is a comma. The rabbinical life
and teachings of Yeshua of Nazareth have been consigned
to a pause, as though he never uttered a word. The Spirit vibrates
in confinement, yearning to release its essence into my life.

The mother and her son's executioner are memorialized
by repetition of their names by worshipers, but of the son's
teachings, not a word is spoken. The splendor of his words
is comma-bound, compressed between compassion and brutality.

What, then, sinks into the Heart? How am I to live? What is
my model, my rule? I cannot be free until I have walked
the precipitous way to Truth and the Light, meditating
on the Master's words, day and night, until they descend
into my Heart, and my life and the teachings become one.

When That behind the teachings opens in my Heart, fear
of judgment will vanish. I may quietly indicate my Heart and say,
It is here. I will know this of myself. It will be discernable
through my actions, without a word from me.

Graffiti

In Paul Green's drama *The Common Glory*
Jefferson sits center stage
at a small table, alone, writing.
His quill, its sound amplified,
scratches across the paper.

He crosses out words and lines
and makes new entries
thinking aloud in amplified whispers:
" ... all men are created equal ... "
" ... certain inalienable rights ... "
" ... life, liberty and property."

He pauses for a long time, deletes
"property" with deliberate strokes
and, accompanied by his own determined,
whispered voice, writes in
" ... the pursuit of happiness."

Extraordinary! Never has a document
by Western political man
contained the language of the Heart.
Jefferson feels this deeply;
it informs every stroke of his pen.

———————————

After two hundred years
we have written property
back in, not with a pen

but a spray-paint can.
We are kids, glossing over
the brickwork in the wall of life.
We have betrayed the revolution.

Low Priority

December; a clear, cold day;
a large office-supply store;
the sales clerk totals my purchases.
Small and efficient, she has
the wrinkles of seventy years.

I pick up my bag of essentials, and say
"Thank you; nice and bright out today."
"Yes," she says, "But it's too cold.
I've worked forty years in this store—
I've never been warm in Maine.
Every winter, I spend three weeks in Florida.
My brother-in-law sends money for the trip.
Isn't that a nice brother-in-law?"
She smiles. I smile, too. "What about
moving to Florida?" Her smile fades,
"There is no plan for retirement here."

A nickel on a pack of pens
a penny on a pencil
applied over forty years
and she could have had a pension
but we, in running about
seeking the lowest price,
cut her out of our minds.

Homo *Faber*

Man rearranges, as in converting
a tree into a table, iron into steel,
or steel into beams, constructs
by connecting beams to raise a tower,
discovers, as in stumbling upon the process
for converting ore into metal
or by mounting telescopes in space
or coring the floor of the sea.

Man receives, as in discerning relationships
between geometric or biological systems
or thoughts and words in metaphor.
In none of these does he create, of himself.
The great discoveries in mathematics and astronomy
are only unfoldings of aspects of the All.

If man creates in imagery, he does not work alone.
Wyeth painted within an image of lace curtains
wafting gently into a bedroom, an indefinable
essence of the scene's true nature,
an impossible expression, a gift from something
… not thingly, an eternal Principle in man.

March 20, 2004

A creature of cold, blue skies
and sun hovering low at noon
a product of memories
lost to this time and place,
I sit in the dark in the kitchen
attempting to enter my inner silence.

Snowflakes distract me
as they swirl, hesitate
and abruptly swarm a streetlight.
This could be the last storm of the season.
I soak up the flakes, store them
against a seven-month drought.

What will I do when earth
resumes its old subtropical nature
after this short subarctic spell?
I'll recycle tropically
become a creature of the sun.

But in this life, I must attend
to things immanent. Over the land today
the warriors celebrated an anniversary,
their conquest of the tyrant of Lilliput
(whose armies dissolved into the sand)
while little knots of those opposed protested.

My desire is to learn to walk
among warriors and protesters
in the Light of the inner silence.
Let me dedicate myself
to this, with all my heart.

Augustine and Einstein

Time flies—where?
When it is gone, where has it gone?
Does it accumulate
like stacks of old newsprint?
Could I riffle it?

Apparently as a moment of grace
or at least, without effort or expectation,
a few have experienced a place
a portion of a town or countryside
as it appeared in centuries past.

Past, therefore, is in store—
still extant in some retrievable way.
What, then, is the meaning of *before*?

Precognition opens *future* to *present*.
Does this invalidate *future*? We are ignorant
of the simplest aspects of the All.

In the conscious mind, time can be
transcendent; in the unconscious
it has no reality at all. What
can we say we know of it?

In near-death experiences, some become
aware of ineffable light; a brightness
passing all understanding. Is this an awareness
of the square of the motion of light?

Can that very backbone of the universe,
the constant through which energy and matter
become one, be experienced?

After the experience, where is the brilliance?
Is it always there, but unperceived
like *past* and *future*? Always where?

Unaccompanied by heat, this inexpressible
light cannot be light as the Sun gives light.
It is not the light of fire. It must be *another* light.

One sees it alone—there are no witnesses;
this light, then, is immanent
and cannot be *other*. It is the Light.
We are the abode of the Light.

What is the abode of *past* and *future*?
If all is within, that is simple enough
on its face, but my mind cannot
grasp it; neither can my mind
embrace nor bring up on command
for my delight *past*, *future*, or the Light.

To fully understand these concepts
it is clear, I must enter their abode
or at least, peer in through the window.
Is the mind the door?
Must I plunge within?
How else can I know?

Valentine Shoppers

A male child, perhaps fourteen, comes around
a counter. His face, remarkably blemish-free,
seems pure, and has the soft, handsome beauty
with which some boys are blessed. The eyes
are kind and bright; the lips smile slightly.

His mother approaches; his forty-year-old twin
though half-a-head taller. She counsels him
closely, patiently, with understanding, on a selection
for someone he is fond of. He listens. Her lips
have his half-smile. Mother and son have been
carefully packaged in complementarity.

A girl, also fourteen or so, notices as her own mother
partly lifts a box from a high shelf. The mother, tall
and large-boned, is quick and gentle in her motions.
The girl, of similar build and demeanor,
has another head taller to grow.

The mother never quite takes down the box
talking all the while, as the girl moves closer
for consultation. They decide against the box
and in flowing motion, turn away
like birds, veering in a flock.

In frequent conversation, punctuated by broad,
soft, open smiles and gentle, heartfelt laughter
the two seem to merge in lightly moving about.
What skill at love has molded, has nurtured this unity?

Contemplating Marion

The eleventh of fifteen siblings on a Nova Scotia farm
where selfless work for the good of the whole gained
an unspoken mark of approval, she grew in the midst
of love and work for all, in a close familial community.

She gained her letters as a British subject, walking
to a one-room school along red-mud paths through
woods and cultivated fields of Annapolis Valley.

She emerged definitely cute, occasionally regal;
given to laughter, self-taught in self-effacement
exceptional in loving kindness, a true friend

overflowing with joyful greetings, pert
hands-crossed-behind-the-back jaunty; a little down
on dark days, but quickly up and humming with the sun.

Sometimes silly when traversing the edge of exuberance,
at times the sage, projecting wisdom—holding it
in her heart. Curious enough about the neighbors, but kind
in her assessment; to her, it is an interest in the marketplace.

Open and thoughtful in offering disagreement;
Fierce in the face of manipulation, but holding
no grievance; Intensely frugal, but once the wherewithal
came into her hands, broadly and carefully generous.

A Bent, descended from John Parker, man of the hour at Concord
she eschewed any attempt to connect with the Daughters
preferring a simple estate and freedom from ostentation.

Educated for nursing in Halifax and later in music in Boston
while a nurse at Peter Bent Brigham, she married John Lundgren
an organist, on his way to Berlin on a fellowship.

For thirty years in Berlin, from just before the Wall went up
until after it came down, she supported her husband
in his music, through long hospital days as a nurse
agreed to have no children to impinge on his dedication
let her piano largely go, and harbored no regrets.
He played in Koblenz, Oberhausen, Berlin and Vienna.
They traveled, knew Europe together.

When his kidneys began to malfunction
she nursed him at home through long, slow hours
of dialysis and a second transplant that failed
before returning to Nova Scotia alone.

After visiting family in West Virginia
perceiving the truth of her sister's health
and staying on through the death
she settled in Maine, and felt at home.

Today, she holds my hand
as we briskly walk in the sun.
Gathered in my palm
is much of the Western world
and the hand of a child of God.

Acceptance

The table supporting my forearms
I accept as ethereal solid. The window
separating me from the rain
brittle ethereal solid or solidified
ethereal fluid, I accept with joy.

Waves of thought, my consciousness
whatever these are, I accept
and myself—I am what I am, but
I cannot express my own reality.

My opinion of consciousness
cannot approach it. Love
may be strangled by the intellect.
I withdraw from my opinions
and desire only to know
and to practice love
beyond intellect and thought
that I may know love absolutely
and in knowing, become and offer it
opening to all that which I am
in the deepest valley of my soul.

Change

A crab apple tree, staunch and full
at peak of blossoming yesterday
today hangs low, wet, half-undressed
its roots under a blanket of petals
like a morning drunk in the park
after a midnight downpour
or a gray-headed woman with auburn hair
disguising her facial lines with makeup
or an old picker and singer
not quite makin' it anymore
in front of his ever-younger audience.

Pigeon Class

On the concourse of North Station
just inside the push-to-open doors
along the street, feet of passengers
pass closely by feet of those in line
at a bagel and donut shop
and the quick, bare feet
of a pigeon warily pecking up
the spilled seeds of everything bagels.
How will he get out of here?

Someone comes too close. The pigeon flutters
around a corner in the three-foot space
between heads and ceiling pipes.
I follow. It is a small waiting area.
Aha! Two birds are pecking here.

I feed Pigeon 1 a bit of egg from the blandest
bagel sandwich on earth. Pigeon 2 moves
to just inside the large glass sliding door
to Tracks 3 and 4, paces back and forth
occasionally stops to peer through the glass
then paces again. Tracks 3 and 4
and the long platforms are empty. No action.

From down the platform, an employee
approaches, with a load on his shoulder.
Pigeon 2 observes, waits. The massive
motion-sensitive door slides aside.

Pigeon 2, apparently sated, walks out
and waddles comfortably along the platform,
like a solitary passenger, to a more
open space and departs on wing.

I want to miss my train, to come back
in the morning and watch a pigeon fly in
flutter up to the door, drop to the platform
as the door opens (as it must at the bird's command)
and walk in for breakfast with solitary dignity.

Bat Mitzvah

Judy became a Jew. Already a Jew
she sealed it through conversion, obviating
the question of her mother's baptism.

The rabbi invited me to basic Judaism classes
to observe, to comprehend the requirements,
the coming changes. I admired Rabbi Cohen.
He presented deeply controversial topics
with humility; a rare gift. He spoke of Jesus
from a Jewish perspective, providing
valuable insight for me, raised Presbyterian.

To this rabbi, I am indebted for a final visit
with my mother. During a Shabbat service
he asked us all to silently meditate and then
to turn our minds to one we had lost. In a moment,
for only a moment, I was in a room with mom;
my gift from the rabbi and the congregation.

Judaism class work done
Judy faced a Bat Mitzvah
in her sixtieth year
while immersed in a struggle
for the survival of her own law practice.
A month before the date, in a conference
the rabbi told her, "You are not ready,"
but Judy insistently kept to the schedule.

On the Bat Mitzvah morning
by Judy's side on the bimah
I was honored to read aloud
a translation of the Torah portion
for the day. I read and stepped aside.
The rabbi remained closely by
to step in if Judy had trouble.

An antique Czechoslovakian Torah scroll
taken from a wrecked synagogue by Nazis
as emblematic of an extinct race
graced a table in front of us.
Addressing the scroll with a pointer
Judy began, not to read, but to chant.
She chanted the ancient Hebrew
the words written without vowels
confidently, without once faltering
her rich contralto filling the sanctuary.
Some in the congregation gazed at her in awe.

I watched in admiration, almost transfixed.
When had she practiced to attain
such mastery? My eyes and posture honored
the intensity of her time of grace
a joyful, communal immersion in Life.

Unity

From Sarasota to New York, from Charleston
to Baltimore to Boston to Bangor
from Virginia to Wyoming, and on to Tomales Bay
from Georgia to Jersey and the Smokies to the sand hills
to the sea, I have known and loved and tried to love
my people; but today, in a theater, the horizons
of my people backed southward against
blue Himalayan ranges, and I moved
in the sand and scrub among shepherds
and camel herders of the Gobi
as they struggled with a camel mare
who refused to suckle her first-born colt.

I became bonded to the Gobis as my own
lived among them, picked up the language
honored the traditions, the ways, let the wind
tear at my heart through the night, knew
the great stillness of the after-storm at dawn
and strained to identify my loved ones
as they approached in the distance on camels
in a mirage of multiple horizons.

The chance to live out this bonding may well escape me
but I attained an understanding of tears in the eyes
of a camel mare on first allowing her first-born colt to
suckle, and never again will I question unity as reality.

A Display of Nineteenth-Century Glass

Silica sand, a product of stars and earth
the stuff of glass for bottles, floods riverbeds
and beaches, but must be blended
with feldspars to enhance the fusion.
These do not survive the rivers and beaches
and must be wrested from the earth.
In parts of New England, antique
feldspar quarries disfigure the forest floor.

For my grandmother's generation, clear glass
perhaps with a touch of green, would not do.
Into the earth went miners, for cobalt, lithium
iron, whatever would mix with glass to enliven
every woman's sideboard with color.

And into the quarries and mines went children.
What was the use of childhood? The key to life
was the work ethic; twelve hours a day
six days a week—no slackers here.
Elegant sideboards blossomed with the lives
of children and their fathers, wasted for a whim.

I stand before locked glass cabinets, absorbing
craftsmanship, free-blown and pressed,
admiring sharp edges of ground-in design
occasional cleverness of pattern
depth or delicacy of color; but I will not
be oblivious of the background brutality.

Flights of Reverberation

On a landing in a semi-Gothic stairwell
a trombone and an alto sax fervently improvise.
Strong wails wrap around long, deep notes
sonorously undulate up and down six flights
of concrete and steel, and echo on all sides
and above and below, from plaster walls
steel doors, floors, risers, treads, windows
and wood, in a remarkable harmony
of overtones and undertones.

The builders did not design for this use
but young musicians have envisioned
and created, in a high-ceilinged
utilitarian stairwell, a cathedral of jazz.

Therapy Session

Last night, as I slept
a siren began to wail, far off.
Prior to my awareness of it
the sound somehow became
an integral part of a dream
that had begun siren-free.

The dream was rewritten
re-enacted during its performance
totally, beginning to end
to seamlessly incorporate the intrusion
as part of the original plot
neatly transcending time.

What door to reality
will you fling wide in the mind
that I may understand this?

Ray Charles

In 1930, the year Gorrell and Carmichael's
"Georgia on My Mind" first appeared on the sheets
Ray Charles Robinson was born in north Florida
which merges imperceptibly with Georgia
the Carolinas and lastly, Virginia
where I was born and raised.

Ray was two years older than I.
His milieu was prohibited to me as a youth
as was mine to him, because his epidermis was dark
and his nose, lips, and hair were not the same
as the features of my family and neighbors.

As an adult, on traverses
along logging roads in the pines
my boots got heavy with Ray's red mud.
I once watched a young black mother
leave her creosoted shack
in a plain cotton dress, her hair
natural in its wooly dreads
and walk in unadulterated beauty
over the same red soil.

I talked with whites about the blacks;
"Something else they don't know is flowers.
They don't know a thing about flowers,"
only to find myself the next day
near the poorest black cabin in the county

its unpainted plank porch deck and railings
alive with cans and pots overflowing with blossoms.

I saw black gangs laboring
under white prison guards with shotguns
but I never saw Ray Charles perform
even though, for forty-five years he set
the world intensely ablaze with his music.

Some place in the midst of this
the glory of "Georgia on My Mind"
became joyfully interwoven
in the deepest fabric of my awareness.
For this, I have known deep gratitude.
I have a debt to Ray.

I have moved north; no more brick-hard
clumps of dried red clay on my boots.
The attitudes of my youth
have largely been transcended.

Yesterday, I absorbed the pain and joy
of Ray Charles' life as it unfolded on the screen.
His genius overrode obstacles
most of us cannot imagine having to face.
And the music—my God, the music!

At the end, I stood, as the credits
began to climb the screen
accompanied by Ray's slow

soulful rendition of "Georgia."

The dam of the sorrows of Ray's people
began to break in my heart.
I leaned against the theater wall for support
wracked with sobbing.

In the ensuing hours, the sobbing
intermittently returned. This morning
though having been unaware of the need
I was led to understand I had been freed.

Recollections of John Harrington

When I was a graduate student, John Harrington retired
as a petroleum geologist and moved to Chapel Hill.
He brought oil-well logs entrusted to him by companies
who knew his genius for pinpointing oil-bearing strata
four miles deep under Gulf of Mexico sand and mud.

John enlivened our seminars by such acts as standing abruptly,
removing his wide leather belt, and contorting it to illustrate
a point. In light of his freedom as a consultant we students
felt imprisoned. John's friendship with Heezen and Tharpe
who charted every valley and ridge and seamount on the floor
of every ocean, touched on the stuff of legend. We were in awe
of John, aware of the contrast between him and faculty who were
secure in the campus womb. As speakers, with John in the room
we figured we damned well better had know our stuff.

John moved to Wofford, as its only professor of geology.
His card now read, "John Harrington, PhD, Geologist and Sage."
On weekend field trips with his students, John drove golf balls
off the Blue Ridge front from a scenic overlook on the Parkway,
talking all the while of the front as a fault scarp. Evenings
in John's motel room were impromptu seminars on life.

As a friend and I rode with John in the southern Appalachians
we stopped for a hitchhiker; twentyish, wearing slacks, a plain
suit coat, a nondescript tie, a Sears white shirt, and an expression
of uncomprehending innocence. We figured he was a student
at one of the Bible Belt colleges, where evolution is the E word.

John introduced my friend and me as geology students, himself as a student of geology, and tried to get a discussion going. The kid didn't take the bait. John didn't press it. It's a delicate procedure, clearing a dust-covered eye.

The Down Drafter

Once I had a wood stove
a square steel box; seamless.
Two short steel tubes
reached inward from the top
adjacent to a round iron lid
on the opening for feeding the fire.

Fires were laid upside down
under each tube,
tinder on top
on kindling on logs
laid flat on yesterday's
fine white ash
in a nest of fire bricks.

Vents above tubes wide open
fire was touched to tinder
the cast iron lid slammed shut
and in a few moments
the view down each tube
was like looking inside
a blowtorch flame—
fire, roaring inward!

Even before the fire box
began to radiate
my heart felt the heat.
A little later, my children
coming down from cold bedrooms
would be swathed in warmth.

Prenatal State

Floating, not needing to breathe
having neither resentment
nor anticipation nor anxiety
nothing to hold or eat
no urge to eliminate or procreate;
floating, in the eternal moment
until we are cast loose
into another environment
of softness mixed with pain and discontent
and awareness of the prenatal state is lost to us
and the longing to return to it
becomes the source of our striving
even without our knowing;
and what we seek
beyond our knowing
is That Which Is, beyond the prenatal;
the eternal goodness of the cosmic womb.

February Sunrise

At 7:40, the cove is a stillness
of pink ice, crumpled at the edges.
Along the nearest shore
a narrow band of turquoise water
between grounded pink ice
and the pink mobile pack
reflects the middle sky
and—what? One of the deep
mysteries of a frigid morning.
No, leave the camera. Let your
mind and Heart absorb and store.

By 9:00, wind and the tide
have closed the turquoise gap.
The pancake of ice is brilliant flat white.
Half a mile away, blue-gray
open water meets the farther shore.
The death grip of January eases.

On the high road across the cove
windows of passing cars
catch the sun and throw it to us.
At night, their headlights
blink among tree limbs
silently, like decorations.

It may not be wise
to live close to the ocean

even on a cove.
One has known hurricanes
reads of tsunamis
but I am staying put.

Timmy Thompson

Prologue

Timmy's town takes up a cape in Maine.
Large homes, some resembling manor houses
some tucked into niches in rock-bound hilly headlands
fill the space between Shore Road and the sea.
Cape Center is inauspicious; a town hall, real estate office
service station, an engine house and a sign by the road
to the high school. Neighborhoods stretch eastward
from the town hall to the sea. Twelve-room homes
border the water. Other homes, each positioned carefully
for an ocean view, dominate low hills behind the shore.

Winter storms can bury cars here, while leaving bare
large arcuate patches of lawn and street. Surf in summer
lulls neighborhoods to sleep, clacking pebbles over cobbles
on a shingle beach. The lure of the water is a presence, always.

Those of us living in the city sometimes cruise the roads
not noticing Timmy's house so much; a large split-level,
an ample space for raising five siblings. We drink in displays
of affluence, offered here without arrogance or embarrassment
and think, perhaps, *here is that which is to be desired.*

Timmy

Here too are demons. Early on, Timmy manifested
the attention deficit hyperactivity demon. In and out
of rooms he went, down and up the stairs, out the door
and in, running and jumping like a wound-up toy.

Had the walls been rubber, he would have been bouncing off.

Stop! His older sisters would say, *Stop!* But for Timmy
just to slow down required sheer will, even under medication.
You might be tempted to sit on him; then you would catch it;
in an instant he would be up and across the room, making funnies,
mirth bubbling up out of a full-faced grin under a shock
of sandy hair, blue eyes sparkling with devilment or kindness
leaving you upside down on the floor, laughing
until you thought your ribs would break.

Who could be angry with him? He always had something
positive to say, some little joke or remark to perk you up
or crack you up, and a smiling, open attitude of at-ease-ness
that took in all around him. In worry or depression
Timmy's friends turned to Timmy; being near him
created a feeling of happiness in you.

What to do with joyful energy in a class room? How to embrace
and redirect boundless enthusiasm? How to concentrate
when your mind goes constantly from here to a zone-free there?
Timmy had his own ways—a friend in front of him in math class,
having indescribable noises directed at the back of her head,
would soon be bent double in laughter. Who was to be disciplined—
Timmy, when he smiled at you,
or put a goofy note to you under an offering of candy,
or squiggled into class, late, on his belly?

Timmy turned eighteen by the end of his senior year. He dropped
the medication for ADHD he had been on since childhood,

saying, "I don't need it anymore;" a familiar refrain to those
who care for ADHD and bipolar patients. No longer medicated
his mind became agitated; sleep and relaxation became difficult.

One morning at sunrise, he parked his truck on a stretch
of sandy beach and went for a long walk. The tide rose.
His beloved Ford pickup, his symbol of himself, was totaled.
No more Mr. Teenaged Mayor, tooling around town
partly hanging out the window, smiling at everyone, "What's up,
Bubby?" He knew them all, and many loved him for it.

He called friends at 3 A.M. on school nights, wanting to hang out,
borrowed friends' cars, raced up and down back roads, horn
blaring, became impulsive and seemed to be in perpetual motion
like his heart wanted to beat right out of his body.
Medications were prescribed; he took himself
off them. He said to a friend, "I'm really depressed."

For years, Timmy's energy had poured over the lacrosse
and soccer fields as unbridled enthusiasm and spirit.
His attitude of always doing his best made deep impressions.
Near graduation, after a final, championship lacrosse game
the opposing coach said, "It was like Tim was trying to put his
whole team on his back to win." But the opposing team won.
Timmy stayed up all night with friends rehashing, crying,
rededicating; "I won't let this stop me. I'm going
to become a better athlete; a better person."

Shortly after, Timmy, his parents and siblings attended a wedding
in Venezuela. Timmy had trouble sleeping; he became confused,

hyperactive, had uncontrollable mood swings and outbursts
of intense energy. On the return trip, Timmy slept through
two long plane rides and in taxis. At the Miami airport, Timmy's
mom was already on the phone to practitioners in Maine.

Back home, Timmy was admitted to a psychiatric hospital.
It was Friday. As the doors locked behind them, Timmy turned
to his parents, terrified, crying, "Why are you doing this to me?
"Why are you leaving me here?" As she left the hospital,
Nancy Thompson, thoroughly scared, asked herself, "How
can this be happening? How did Timmy get so sick so fast?"
By Monday, all signs of manic behavior were gone. Timmy
seemed to be Timmy. The staff saw no reason now to keep him.

Timmy entered a program for treatment of bipolar, incipiently
psychotic or suicidal teens. His parents filled out forms laying out
the family's mental health history. In the initial interview
the counselor turned to Timmy, "Are you suicidal?" To Nancy
the question was like a blow to the heart; "Why is he asking
Timmy this?" Timmy's reply was adamant: he had never had
such thoughts. He agreed to take a mood-stabilizing drug
but took himself off it soon after. He called the counselor aside
before leaving and confided, "I'm depressed."

On July 23, in a three-hour therapy session Timmy learned
how his deck was stacked: a bipolar cousin on each side;
his father's brother in Montana, bipolar, had spent several years
in a psychiatric ward, and now lived in a group home.

On July 24, a Saturday, at Timmy's request a bedroom switch

was made; Timmy moved upstairs out of the basement
(*It's too dark down there.*); his brother moved down. His sisters and
mom busied themselves rearranging, hanging new curtains. Timmy
kept to himself, roamed the house, retreated
to the bathroom. His sisters knocked a couple of times,
"You OK?" "Yeah, it's just some bad stomach thing."
On one excursion out of the bathroom, Timmy hugged
his mom, "I love you, mom." On another, "Dad,
I feel like I'm losing my mind; my thoughts are racing."

In late afternoon, Timmy's dad returned from an errand
and checked on Timmy, still in the bathroom. Minutes later,
there was a large boom. His dad raced back. Timmy
lay against the tub. *My God, he's fallen and hit his head.*
Then Tim saw the pistol in the sink. Purchased months before
to protect the office, then found needless, it had been secreted
in the house, weapon in one place, cartridges in another.
Timmy had found both. *Lead me from the unreal to the real.*
Lead me from this darkness into Light.

The news spread almost immediately, from the neighborhoods
to the town hall to the cove, miles away, the favorite
gathering place for teens. Timmy's good friend Rex found
his own parents and brother weeping in the car. Told the reason
he shouted at his parents, "No! No! No!" Colin, another
close friend, dropped his cell phone, felt sick and angry
went out of the house and screamed. Meaghan, down at the cove,
began to shake, crying uncontrollably. She had grown up
with Timmy. *I could always count on him to make me smile*
when I was down. How could he have shot himself?

Others had thoughts of their own:
Timmy was just the happiest kid I ever knew.
He was a huge part of all of our lives.
He was always there for us.
No one will ever be the same.
Why didn't he say something to us?

He did. He said, "I'm depressed." It was the loudest
sound he ever made, but our minds did not want to hear
or follow the implications before the fact.

Epilogue
Tim and Nancy Thompson, having had their oldest son
taken out of life by his own hand, opened their hearts
to the world. Three days after Timmy's death, in the midst of shock
and grief, Nancy assembled counselors from the
Center for Grieving Children at the Cape Community
Center to minister to three hundred of Timmy's friends
and their families who packed the hall. Tim Thompson spoke;
I am not ashamed of my son. He was taken away by an illness.
Depression killed him. Tim's voice broke
again and again as he urged them all to learn
to deal openly with the hidden demon of depression.

In their vulnerability, many of Timmy's friends grasped
Tim's courage and held it close, saw how he reached out
to them through his pain, and would remember.

In September, Tim and Nancy were at the soccer fields

as in seasons before, cheering on their own children
and inviting Timmy's friends over after. Nancy said
quietly but firmly to herself, *I'm here for them.*

The anniversary of Timmy's death approached. Uncertain
what to do, Tim and Nancy made the move that seemed right
for them; a cook-out was scheduled. The Thompson's back yard
filled with Timmy's friends and relatives. Nancy wore Timmy's
favorite soccer shirt. Tim's shirt was designed by a local coach
to keep the memory of Timmy alive in the minds of Cape players;
YOU WILL NEVER WALK ALONE. Tim and Nancy greeted
everyone like the old friends they were. Tim continued
his campaign; *When you have cancer, people bring you
a casserole. If you have bipolar disease
or depression, no one wants to come near you.*

Mostly, people remembered Timmy as a living attitude
of positiveness, a catalyst for a chain reaction of positive
thoughts and actions. At this cook-out, a year-time celebration
of life in death, little weeping was heard, and no lamentation.

Morning Event

Gulls! Gulls! Gulls!
slowly and skillfully circling

Hreeer!   Hreeer!

        Hreeer!

                Hreeer! Hreeer!

the initial sound neither a hard *h* nor a soft *k*
but the sound of the throat, opening,
the long double *e* very shrill,
the sounds hovering among gliding wings
celebrating unity with water and air.

Hreeer! Hreeer! Hreeer!

                Hreeer!

What could be more joyful?
Unable to circle aloft
a gull among gulls
I do not know.

The question could be answered
in a conference with gulls
if one could find translators, but
analysis is a dead fish.

Enjoy! Enjoy! Enjoy!

Grace

One night ten years ago, and one night only
for a moment at the limen of sleep
I became aware of being curled up
softly in the lap of the Lord.
Never have I known such sweetness.

I tried to reenter that space.
The intellect could not bridge the gap
whatever the gap may be.
I became soon aware
that applying the intellect
in this way storms the gates.

Since then, I have waited for grace.
But for an occasional suffusion with joy
little has been consciously given. Glimpses
are what I have known of heaven.

Recollections of joy drive me to prepare,
to watch, so that, when near enough
to the arms of love, I may be enfolded.

When am I near enough to know?
When am I far enough away
to be not drawn in?

Dinner at the Brunswick Diner

Looking for an old haunt
for dinner in Brunswick
we can't find it, turn a corner to leave
and there, just a couple of blocks
down old Route 1, we see a sign
sort of in somebody's yard
—DINER—The Brunswick
"good home cooking
at a down-home good price"
Breakfast All Day Since 1946
A happy discovery. We go in.

It's a diner: arched ceiling, long counter;
anchored chromed-steel stools with rotating tops
photos and plaques on the back wall
and booths for four along the outside.
We take a booth. The waitress, thirty-five
or forty, comfortable, subtly rumpled
has a born-in-the-neighborhood look.
The menu is meat-and-potatoes
lobster, clams, crab, and sides.

With low expectations, we ask,
"Do you have anything for vegetarians?"
"Oh, sure—it's new, not on the menu yet—
stir-fried vegetables topped with cheese."
"Oh, we'd like that. May we have two orders
please, and two cups of joe, one decaf."

(Why did I say "joe"?) We wait and peruse.

Antique cartons of unopened Coke
decorate high shelves on the end walls.
At one end stands a vintage
Wurlitzer, with racks of vinyls
and painted-glass neon panels.
"Oh, man, look at this." (Flippable flaps
that have song titles on paper slips)
"We could play, "Between the Sheets"
and, "With No Pants On." Golden
oldies ourselves, we like this place.

The menu has photos and a history:
It's a Worcester diner car, sold in the thirties
to its first owner, in western Maine;
christened the Norway Diner
later the Norwaygo, then moved east.
In '46, it became the Miss Brunswick.

Our coffee arrives. I load my decaf
with sugar and half and half and start to stir.
Three guys in dark-blue Dickies, looking a bit worn
slide into the next booth. The waitress brings coffee
without being asked. They perk up, begin to enjoy
each other; joke with the waitress.
These men have been here forever.
Our veggies arrive, more than enough.
We dig into the piles; first-rate stuff.

On the way out, I pick up a menu
seek out the waitress, point to the history.
"Do you have this on a card to give out?"
"No," she says, pleased at the interest,
"But just a minute." She enters the kitchen
and comes right out with a slightly spotted
photocopy of the menu. "You can have this."
One last look around and we leave.
"She gave us the cook's copy?"
"I think so." We hug as we walk.

American Legacy
A Newspaper Collage

I

In Baghdad, American soldiers, seeking insurgents
smash inward the outward-opening wooden door
of a small stone house, revealing an Iraqi girl of fifteen
holding a younger sibling, and raising her free hand
in intense fear, as though to ward off the crushing blows.

II

Darkness rises at Tall Afar. The curfew approaches.
Hussein Hassan hurriedly drives the family Opel
with his wife Kamila at his side and five
of their seven children squeezed into the back seat.

Twelve-year-old Rakan spots an impromptu
road block of soldiers, but too late to voice a warning.
A fusillade of bullets from half-a-dozen-guns
tears up the front half of the car, spattering the children
with a mixture of glass and their parents' blood.

The car rolls to a stop. Rakan tries to run, but cannot;
his lower spinal column shattered, his legs don't work:
In fifteen seconds, two dead, seven orphans and a cripple.
Four small children climb out of the car, wailing.
They crouch in semi-darkness among guns and booted feet.
A soldier offers candy. The children wail and refuse.

The soldiers' captain verbally absolves them

of any wrongdoing, but that will not quell
the recurring dreams of the soldiers or their victims.

III

In a Shiite town to the north, teenaged American men
in uniform, with automatic weapons, joke with Iraqi boys
in whatever way you can joke with boys who speak
another language in a context beyond your ken.

These boys do not know the Amis in the role
they have adopted on assignment in Iraq:
trackers and killers of men; terrifiers
killers and maimers of the innocent.

Ruth Farabee Clark

seldom far from the local stage as a performer
was always up for any role. She reached out
and touched everyone she stood before
with an uncommon sense of what an audience
needed, whether it was a theater of people
or you, standing next to her in a room.

Hospitals were her second abode.
It began with childhood diabetes and progressed
through kidney transplants and heart attacks
but you had to be close in before
she would confide anything about her health.

On hearing of another illness, Ruth's associates
would say, *Yeah? OK, she's in the hospital now*
but she'll be at rehearsal tonight.
On reporting to the stage, it would be,
"Here I am. Block me. Where do you want me?"
with no reference to how she had spent her day.

Asked why she threw herself completely
into roles, Ruth replied, "Because I really
don't know how much time I've got.
I don't want to take a chance
on missing anything. When I go, I know
I will have done everything I wanted to do."

A week before her final performance, she returned

to her family home. "It's time," she said.
Her bed was arranged in the living room.
Friends and family visited; some sang
from her favorite roles. The house was full
of spirit and song. "It's sad," Ruth said,
"planning my own funeral – I won't be there."

But she was the star of the show
and had the best seat in the house.

Darkness and Light

Sunday Morning
Klik—clank! A steel door opens.
My foster son enters a closet-sized room
and sits. Discordant voices in argument
from corridors of a granite-block jail
resound through the open door.
The door slams, leaving echoes.

I sit in the adjoining closet. The boy and I
do a knuckle press through heavy glass.
We converse through a slit.
He appears to be at his best, calm
smiling, reasonable, raising my spirits.
Later, on the phone, he tells me the crux
of his comments had been untrue.

In the bowels of human existence
displaying a sincere, engaging smile
like the pleasantest fellow in the world
he had lied. It is possible to sink lower
but I don't want to imagine it
relative to this boy.

Every rung he tries on the climb
out of the pit of his life collapses
when he missteps, mishears
overshoots, lunges at the unperceived
fragility of the ladder, or

relies on the sand foundations
of relationships built on lies.
 … But this time, he did own up …

Tuesday Evening
Fifty miles away, Stephanie Chase, violinist
with the apparent ease that accompanies
great virtuosity, explores the heights
and depths of that remarkable structure
Beethoven's Concerto in D Major, while performing
in another remarkable structure, an antique
granite-block auditorium recreated as a concert hall.
Cacophony has been filtered out by sound baffles
that rise to impressive heights and flare out
to encompass the audience. Stephanie, Beethoven
and the orchestra, striving toward Truth
celebrate the highest image of the human.

I sit enraptured in the loge
an insignificant daub of pink and grey.
Had Stephanie looked at me in performing
our Hearts might have met in a press
of air inlaid with music. She converses
with me through her fiddle and bow
as her body re-expresses the music
subtly, through its own language.

Here are flights of soul
to unimaginable inward heights
that my son might experience in his cell

like a monk, if he strode an inward
way to open himself to grace.

But, now, the glass between him
and Stephanie is thick, and I do not know
whether he can see through darkly, or at all.

Mind Power

An Argument

Walking on a road above low cliffs on the Atlantic
my eyes on macadam, I became aware
of being directly linked through Panama
with friends in California. My mind then displaced
the road in my central vision with an equally vivid image
of linear, low mountain ranges, blue in the distance
from a perspective of thousands of feet aloft.
From an effulgence in a valley between two ridges
Roman candle-like flares arced aloft. In my peripheral
vision, macadam still passed beneath my feet.

The mind had overcome itself, replacing an image
of reflected daylight with an internal image
in accordance with the will of a presence
consciously unknown to me; unknown
if not known, because of my limited awareness.
The inference was clear: The ashram near Tomales
sends out variegated messages from the effulgence
of the master's teachings. This was not new
to me, but the portrayal as fireworks brought
a sense of immediacy, inwardly urging me onward.

Later in the year, I traveled with friends to Tomales.
Just west of Petaluma, at a high section of road
blue ridges of the coastal ranges dominate the horizon.
I knew them at once as the ridges of my vision in the east.

Beside the Atlantic, my mind had projected an image
of that which *is not* there, but *is* here. Only the fireworks
could be called hallucinatory, but they cannot be
distinguished from an ordinary dream; a visualized
thought formation that overrode images cast by daylight.

By what internal power was the central image overcome?
What discretionary dynamic allowed the peripheral image
to remain?—Or was it merely an oversight, a cobweb
left in the corners? This process is part of my system.
Can I open my awareness to include it? Why should I?
Such ruminations lead to nothing.
Accept the message with gratitude.
Leave extraneous ocular effects alone.

The Pulling

Evening at the Annapolis Valley Exposition: the fiddling
was dispirited, automatic. Guitars followed, a mix of acoustic
and electric, all country, all the same, led by a lame MC.
I had to exit, took a side door, across a little way of gravel,
not wanting to turn right to BATHROOMS, and was
stopped by a high black lattice—the underside of a grandstand.
Through the openings, between ankles and calves, bright light
revealed an opposing grandstand and a central way of dry
hard-packed soil. A wooden sled loaded with six-foot, four-sided
prisms of concrete, rugged and ominous, sat behind a team
of brown stallions. The horses, massive, closely curried,
tails trimmed short, in polished harness with chrome studs,
waited restlessly. A loud speaker announced, "12,000 kilograms;"
a 13-ton truck on skids. The teamster, a farmer of moderate size,
his work horses up for a power display, seemed dwarfed
by the sleek haunches. With hard words and strong pulls
on the reins he positioned and restrained the horses, even daring
to push a haunch forward from behind. One stallion, his neck
curved strongly downward, pawed the ground with his great
right hoof in towering impatience. The sense of challenge
was palpable and made audible in the pawing, tossing of heads
and jangling harness. The teamster worked to rein in impatience
but not diminish desire. At the instant of shouted command
two rippling engines strained forward with intense determination,
absolute concentration and legendary power. The sled-bound mass
moved a meter, a meter and a half, and stopped. The horses swayed,
steaming. A meter stick was laid out. An announcement was made in
the midst of clapping. The teamster unhitched

the horses and gently urged them out of the pulling shed.
They slowly pranced in precise unison toward the parking lot, trailed
by the reins held by the teamster, who leaned a little back so that his
booted feet hit the ground flat, without style
like the paws of a creature from a planet of sloths.

In a Photograph

my mother, at twenty
holds her firstborn infant
my sister, now eighty-six
and looks toward her
with tender fascination
open acceptance, wonder,
determination to fulfill her duty
and the dedication of one
who chose marriage over college
and did not look back. Thus,
thirteen years and two children later
I was allowed to manifest.

Had I been an observer
at the scene of the photograph
a neighbor or passing stranger
I would have smiled to myself,
What a privilege it would be
to grow up as a child
of that young woman.
And so it was.

Sketch

Riffles of air manifest as ripples
in moving over the lake
and intersect a flock of sitting gulls.

Two gulls take flight astride the wind.
The others follow, leaving the lake
to riffles of air and migrating
congregations of ripples.

Heather Marie, at Sixteen

On a Sunday morning, Heather approaches a lectern
in the center of a circular sanctuary.
In childlike innocence, she slowly bows
in reverence before the altar, prays,
Dear God, I sing for you,
and positions herself before a microphone.

All eyes are on her; a few are anxious
or expectant, but all wait.
Children who know her are in awe.
She diverts her eyes to one side
a trait of her autism, addresses her entire self
to a psalm set as a song, a song she knows,
having listened to it once with unwavering attention.
Her focus is absolute. Unmindful of herself
she lets her hands do what they will, and sings
sweetly, perfectly on pitch, precisely in time
in deep reverence for cantoring, for leading others
to prayer. After years of therapy and determined
practice, Heather modulates her volume well.

As a child, in the park, Heather said to her parents,
"God is sitting on that bench over there," but they
saw only a homeless man. Heather's explanation:
"I see God in everyone." As did Francesco of Assisi
Ramana Maharshi and others who have known
That Which Is within. "God lives in people,"
says Heather. "We should treat people like they are God."

In the hall at school, between classes, a schoolmate
who has noted Heather's difficulty with speech
sees Heather's free hand hanging, inclined
to the rear from the wrist, the slight
forward slump of her body, and her eyes
cast to one side to avoid contact, and attacks,

"Hey, girl, are you stupid or retarded?"
"I'm Heather," says Heather, and flings
her arms around the girl's neck, saying,
"I'm sorry you're having a bad day.
I'll pray for you." The girl is dumbfounded,
"Didn't you hear me? I called you a loser."
"I know," says Heather, "but I love you."
She smiles her full smile, which, when offered
to one she loves, such as you, becomes
infused with the joy of the Lord; and Heather
becomes a vessel of love, brimming.

In drama class in September, a new classmate
gripes, "Heather is always complimenting people,
happy all the time. Nobody can be that nice.
She's a fake." By December, the tune has changed.
"Heather is awesome; she doesn't think ugly
or pretty. She has a reverence for you as you.
She makes sure nobody is left out, even
someone who doesn't like her, like me.

"When I realized Heather is for real, I fell for her.

The least good we do she lets us know
she appreciates what we're doing. She tells us
we're beautiful, which makes us stop and ponder
because she is the one who is beautiful."

The Tower of Emptiness

To direct our attention
from vast inner realms
to obscure their existence
a spire of remarkable height and grace
will rise at the site of the WTC
from the sad little hole that remains.

I stand at the rim of this scar
a dimple on the edge of the Atlantic
and imagine other scenarios;
a sunken park and gardens
horses for riding and loving
a skating pond kept frozen
from Christmas to Presidents' Day.

We could buy the land, we
the people, and keep it
for ourselves, do with it what we wanted
keep it green, a memorial to those
we lost, a reminder to ourselves that
despite this green spot of rightness
something is wrong in the world.

But no, the already-targeted tower
will rise, reaching toward nothing.
It is just what we wanted, mostly
not a garden of introspection
in which to cultivate silent strength

but a tower whose glitter will confirm
for a time, Merton's complaint in the thirties
that drove him into the monastery;
we have no interior life.
Nothing is what we have learned.

Rule: Ahimsa Paramo Dharma

An American Antithesis, 2004

To be not passive. To seek a quiet state of mind
free from anger, a positive state of love,
of doing no harm or wrong, even to the wrongdoer.

To submit to no injustice; to bear no ill will
toward any living creature. To gently but firmly
resist the wrongdoer by all nonviolent means
neither giving offense, nor giving way.
To conquer untruth by truth;
in resisting untruth, to put up with all suffering.

Never to waiver in the resolve to live in truth
and to realize the truth of the scriptures.
To speak truth to my peers and to power
letting my "Yes" be yes and my "No" be no.

To be fearless and pure and detached from material things;
to take joy in renunciation. To desire nothing for myself.
To empty myself of myself, and live for the joy of others.
To strive to attain the end of sorrow.

To be full of the desire to serve.
To give of myself freely
as though it were my own nature.
To serve both friend and foe with equal love.

To act in love, putting first always the welfare of the whole.

To show good will to all, being mindful of that which is noble
in the sight of all. To be compassion in action.

To learn to walk in humility, through knowing my Self as I am.
To be pure in heart, free from lust and the sense of *I* and *mine*.
To be pure in mind, so that thoughts I do not approve cannot arise.
To purify my light, that it may be seen by all who can see.

To assuage my anger, and remove the logs and lust from
my own eye, by repeating always the prayer of the holy name
and being reconciled with my brother or sister.
To open my heart to anyone who harms me;
to give of myself to him in light of his need
and to walk in love an extra mile with a hard overseer
that my detachment may become complete.

To know that anyone who calls me enemy
is a vessel for the divine seed
of That which is in all, and to pray for him
letting a holy name or phrase flow over him in love.

To deepen my humility
by letting my kindnesses be known
only to those who receive them.

To practice stillness of body and mind
so That which is perfect may reveal itself in me.
To constantly and silently practice, in private places
and in the market, the prayer of the holy name.

To live in consonance with the word.
To forgive, that I may be forgiven.
To love, that I may love.
To store up treasures only in the heart.

To be nonjudgmental and thus non-injurious.
To withdraw my attention from yesterday
and tomorrow and live in awareness of
the moment, free from resentment and anxiety.

To seek first That Which Is, as it is
without preconception or expectation.
To sit in silence, that I may discern
and act upon the will of the Lord.

Part 2
*Poems from May 2006
through October 2008*

Rehearsal

The empty clack of the fork on the plate.
No one else breathing when I lie still.
Silence in place of your humming
your laughing at trifles; your busyness.
You are due back in two days
but this taste of aloneness is to my distaste.

I need no rehearsal of loss.
When it is time, we go.
You may go first or I
but out of a vortex of hundreds of lives
slowly, effortlessly turning
will come you and me and a gain.

That Which Is

In our categorizing, our desire
to hold infinity in the palm of the hand
and examine it, determine its parts
which it does not have, being all,
and in each, beyond comprehension,
we attempt to limit the boundless
That, inherent in itself as it is,
eternal, immutable, self-aware
consciousness, "the transcendent reality
without name or form, beyond
the reach of feeling and of thought."

In *The Tao of Physics,* Capra implies,
the unity of all reality is inherent
in all that is by virtue of its nature.
When all that is coheres as a universe
unitary consciousness inheres in it
as That we address in our ignorance as Lord.

We can sense that the whole
is greater than the sum of its parts
though being aware in our daily rounds
of parts alone. It is this ignorance,
this limited awareness
we must transcend, each of us,
one by one, to stand before/within
That Which Is as coevolutionary, as one.

Family

Thanksgiving Day; in a small apartment,
a table set for four. The guests arrive
a mother and daughter, sixty-eight
and thirty-three, the mother from fifty
miles north, her daughter from a borough
of New York. The mother brings
chardonnay and rich vegetarian desserts.

The hosts, the father and his wife
seventy-four and seventy-nine
their grayness earned apart
have not been together long.
The wife greets the daughter joyfully
her mother cordially, with great
appreciation for her offerings, one by one.

The chardonnay is offered as a toast
around the table to togetherness.
The hosts arrange dishes on the stove;
candied yams and tofu pot pie.
The late autumn day dies rapidly
outside a triple window on a cove.

All serve themselves, as the conversation
migrates to and from and around the table
and settles in. Absent offspring
of the mother and father are remembered
in turn as the talk might turn to them.

A daughter, thirty-one, the twin of her mother's mother
as a teen, who approaches life with her mother's
compassion, is called in northern California.
The phone is passed around in animated conversation.

An adopted son, thirty-five, who makes music
with his band in Los Angeles, settled deeply
into his songs and musicianship, has drifted away.
Two other daughters of the mother, forty-two
and forty-seven, step-children of the father,
are not called, nor is a foster son, twenty-three,
under court order to stay away from the mother.

The wife has remained childless, by choice.
The father has experienced the barbs
of acrimonious divorce, and sees
the disturbance in a daughter, forty-six,
who has absented herself
from this gathering, in the face of her
intermittent anguish, that stems
from inherited tendencies
and years of negative abuse
from her own mother, whose last ten years
were spent in isolation, after her daughter
chose not to speak with her. After the passing
the daughter came finally to know
forgiveness for her mother and herself.

Side by side with this daughter

the father knew pain in the lengthy
dissolution of a misguided union,
but she grew to wade into large chunks of life
bringing hearty, infectious laughter
and ready acceptance of unknown faces
of subtly-recognized souls.

An elephant of the father's own making
is in the room, his abusive behavior
toward the stepdaughters as children.
The daughters have long since forgiven him
though a subtle leeriness remains.
Today, this elephant seems small.

In early evening, dishes to take home are packed.
The wife and the mother embrace, warmly.
The host hugs his daughter
who closely resembles his own mother
but is prettier, and seems as wise.

The mother approaches the father, smiling
confidently, takes his arm closely
and turns her right cheek to receive his kiss.
The father, quietly a little stunned
proffers the kiss, but remains silent,
needing time to absorb the scene
which he contemplates during the evening
and following morning, until he understands
that in the turning of the cheek
was forgiveness he had never hoped to know.

Speculation

If mind is waves of thought
there are no boundaries, but perhaps
a gradual fading to stillness
like waves among reeds in marsh.
No, thought waves must be friction-free;
(What would rub against what?)
there can be no diminution.

Thought waves, subtle, accessible
formations in boundless four-dimensional
reality, merge or intermingle with no
interference, and permeate the universe.

Over or through what medium
do thought waves travel?
On what shore do they break?
The analogy begins to crumble.

Some thought formations
are possibilities, some irrational;
the intellect must discriminate.
Passing thoughts can be
dispassionately observed, but why
am I aware of my thoughts alone?
I could observe your thoughts
perhaps, in absolute stillness …
but "The stilled mind is
universal spirit;" free of thought.

When a mind is stilled,
thoughts no longer are to it
but thoughts still are
the unstilled minds about it.
Near a stilled mind, thoughts
tend to be drawn down
a thought sink, yielding calmness.

What boundaries among thoughts
keep mine from entering yours?
Schrödinger says, none. "The sum total
of the number of minds in the universe
is one." Nevertheless, your thoughts
appear to be blocked from mine;
off-limits by subconscious preconditioning
like memories or awareness of other lives.
Mind and *my thoughts* are not the same.

My thoughts insist,
There must be a boundary,
but cannot come up with one.
They fail to perceive thought's limits
and thus appear to have
no experiential knowledge of mind.

.

Stilling my mind will not still yours,
so there is a separation, an estrangement.
We are back to the word *mind,*
with little understanding

of the reality it represents
except that my mind
(or my awareness of mind)
can be gently removed from the riotous
circus of thoughts, and then, as may be said,
my mind will have been annihilated.

Then there will be for me
no need to utilize mind
nor any meaning in the word
unless I chose to be mindful.

Best we dispassionately let
the unfathomable concept, *mind,*
pass by; a thought to be let go of. Yet,
how can mind be unfathomable, unthinkable?
Here is mind again, arising—
a dragon, to be slain.

Street Ball

A volleyball, one dad
three stair-step kids, twelve to six
two girls and a boy in the middle;
a seam in macadam for a net.

They make the rules.
The older girl
an eye on dad's approval
serves gamely.
The boy returns it, sort of
but has to chase it himself
out of indefinite bounds.

The little one
awed a little by the ball
seems to be having
her first game.

The dad smiles
laughs a bit of fun into it
plays with or at each child
mindful of personalities,
levels of ability
and creates a harmony.

They have turned macadam

into magic; a segment of a morning
into a momentous event.
They leave for lunch
taking with them memories
for weaving their lives into a whole.

Healing the Thumb

Folded wooden table under arm, I stumbled
up the two steps to my daughter's place.
All went sprawling—my thumb impressed itself
along a spring-steel band beneath the table top,
laying open a 3/4 by 1/4-inch flap of skin
      and a linear cut beyond the joint.

I held the thumb head high until the bleeding stopped
and drove home one-handed, thumb up and tissue-wrapped.
Resident nurse Marion applied a squeeze of ointment
      and two one-inch Band-Aids.

The blood cells, having worked quickly
and well to coagulate, sacrificing thousands
      in wiped-away over-coagulation
(in the manner of excess acorns crowding the base of an oak
or ungathered dust and gases in a galaxy after star birth)
moved on to other duties. The skin flap seemed
too big to save, but blood and skin cells knew the work
      and had already set about it.

Next morning, the skin flap's white jagged edge
was matched, irregularity by irregularity,
by a dead white rim of skin across a chasm
      the width of a thousand cells.

In two days, the chasm was closed, its edges tightly knit
to new tissue, no gaps, no leaks, jagged edges

jumbled aside, out of the way of the workforce.
The skin flap, its lower portion now over fluid called up
from glandular recesses, was sensitive, like a pink blister.

Coagulation, construction of new tissue, the efficient
sealing of the wound, all were accomplished quickly
as work for the good of the whole, in which
        coordination replaced rivalry
without question or argument, following procedures
worked through and honed by billions of cell generations
        since the earliest beginnings.

The cells behave like creatures having awareness,
        partaking in consciousness.
We deny this, not wanting to admit that cells
        may be aware as we are aware
        or have a communal awareness,
interacting, interpenetrating, living, working, dying,
        in response to trouble
or yielding to routine in the vast
interior communities of themselves.

My Daddy Passes Closely By

I

I visited him in the hospital.
He was seventy-nine. We smiled,
him especially. I took his hands,
more warmly and happily
than ever before. He was
very proud of me (Mom said),
of my PhD and teaching, the first
in his German immigrant family.
The more serious travesties in my life
of which he would have been ashamed
had not been revealed then. He knows now,
though, in the after-death knowing.

A few weeks after the hospital visit
my sister said into the early-morning phone,
"Daddy's gone." All I could say was, "Oh,"
not having been closely attached
or drawn to him after childhood
and having been trained to be
publicly unfeeling ("Boys don't cry,
don't hug"), and being somehow
not greatly affected by his death.

I remember standing at the head
of the basement stairs. "Daddy, watcha doin'?"
"I'm paint'n'." Down I would go, to watch
and mess around, or perhaps be allowed

to spread a little paint. In this way,
I learned early on to handle and care for a paint brush,
drive a nail, make a recovery, using only the hammer
when a nail flared to the side, or straighten a bent nail
on a wood block, skills that have enriched my life.

Quiet at home, Daddy read much
out of shelves packed with Book of the Month
Club novels and biography, Southern
Civil War history, the likes of Max Brand,
and an encyclopedia of vocal music.
He was a regular church-choir tenor.

His philosophy was simple, "Live and let live,"
a great stabilizing influence.
Salesman, sales manager, then president
of a wholesale mill-supply house
his work seemed distant from me.

At social gatherings with fellow Rotarians,
he was affable, "hail-fellow-well-met,"
but in unwinding with friends
in the Acca Temple Chanters,
silliness sometimes took over, almost
to the point of becoming unglued.
This could go on for hours.

My brother and I, puzzled and disappointed,
confronted Mom about this, after a day-long
men-only fishing trip. "Daddy seems not

to have his feet on the ground." We needed
to unload, but what could she say or do?

What could we expect of a man
who spent his life fully engaged in work
he didn't like? His decades-long problem
with migraines cleared up soon after he retired.
What condition would I have been in at that point?
I spent my life working in accordance with
my own lights, beginning with the college time
Daddy's dedication bought and paid for.

                    II
Daddy seemed to be an uncomplicated man
who lead a simple life, with a good bit
of affluence toward the end of his working.
During the night after I began this poem,
I dreamed vividly of removing layer after layer
of peeling, variegated porch-and-deck paint
from the outside walls of an A-frame attic,
the simplest possible covered structure,
even uncovering a painted-over screen door,
but never getting down to the original
unpainted surface of heart-pine lumber.
So much for the simple man.

Even today, on the older homes
you can drive a nail into heart-pine clapboards
only with difficulty. Such lumber
was still being milled when Dad first

called on sawmills in rural Virginia
and North Carolina. Clear-cutting this timber
was akin to cutting the heart out of the country,
but Dad and the lumbermen thought of it
as supplying the growing needs of a nation.
Heart pine embodies the quality of Dad's life.

III

In a repatterning session, I was asked to contemplate
my remembrances of occasionally going down
for the night or waking in the big bed in my
older sister's bedroom. I have had dreams
of sleeping there. Surely, it was because I was born
early in her fifteenth year, and when I was four
she left for college, like my second mother, going away.

Similar to Mom in appearance and demeanor
she would have been a youthful image
of Dad's bride in the house. Becoming aware
of this aspect of his life has made Dad
more human to me, more approachable,
man-to-man. His rare little quirky times
of repeatedly verbalizing bad puns
fall quietly into place. His life becomes
beyond judgment by the likes of me.
My love for him grows. Finally, I miss him.

In Passing

Three bright leaves
on a bare twig of maple;
the yellow flowers of November.

Shall I take one
and press it?
Remember Blake
and kiss it
en passant.

A Replacement for Hanley Denning

I saw her briefly, once. She spoke to us
at the university of her mission
to the garbage-picking children
of the great dump at Guatemala City;
her desire to get them out of the dump
and into public schools
or educational centers for tutoring
and early childhood development,
hot meals and medical attention,
centers established near the dump
by herself and her group of one hundred
staffers and four hundred volunteers,
that had grown in six years from herself alone.

In less than a year, she was gone
cut down by an overturning truck;
the children, their mothers, staffers
and volunteers, all stunned.

An interim director was appointed;
in the midst of grief; the search
for a replacement was begun.
Said a co-chair of the board,
"We're pretty sure about the mission,
but we'll never find another Hanley."

Why not? Her willingness to turn her back
on an affluent life to live among the poorest

of the poor, and dedicate her very self
to their wellbeing, was this unique?
No. We all have this capacity,
however deeply hidden.
I am the replacement for Hanley Denning
and you, and you. What is holding us back?

Gleanings and Giftings

I cannot walk the Way of the Cross
but must seek other ways, unassigned.
In long pauses by Nhat Hanh and Eknath
Easwaran, speaking in video
I sense the movement of That in them.

Reading from commentaries by Easwaran
on the Gita, I enter familiar sections
in which I know he will approach Truth
as closely as words can take us.
Willingness to leap into the unknown
stirs within me, releasing joyful sorrow
from the depths of the Self, and I must wait
to be sufficiently composed to continue.

In my room, reading of questions posed
by visitors to Bhagavan Ramana Maharshi,
his replies, small acts of maintenance
or devotion by his devotees and staff,
descriptions of where he walked,
my mind transforms to deep longing,
an intense craving for grace.
Later, walking about on the business of the day,
I become aware of a subtle emptiness, a hunger.
I stop, slowly repeat the mantrum
and momentarily sink into subtle peace.

In the teachings of that radical

of radicals, Yeshua of Nazareth
I see and desire to travel
the long hard road to Truth.

Once a year, twenty-five miles south
Father Ed McLean, old veteran
of the wars within the heart
the struggle for peace, prayer,
and the deep silent waiting,
speaks to a room full of us
gathered in retreat. His voice
and demeanor at times reflect
utter stillness; the deep inner silence
Merton urges us to enter.

"We don't understand God,"
says Father Ed, "We experience him."
The words come calmly, slowly, intensely,
out of that place that is no place
in which the scriptures arise.

Daily, seventy miles north
an autistic young woman
sees God in all around her.
What does she see?
The glory of That Which Is
inherent in us all.

I thought I could ask no more of the Presence,
the indivisible unity, than these

widely-flung gleanings and giftings,
doorways fleetingly opening on That;

But yesterday, following on years
of faltering concentration in meditation
and facing down discouragement at the door,
I sat alone in the living room facing
the piano wall. For a few moments
I became aware that my mind was still.

A sense of enormous expansiveness
merged with the stillness, and I realized
I was observing everything internal and external
in absolute dispassion. My acceptance
of the reality of stillness of mind
passed beyond faith into knowledge.

A Black and White Llama

in its stall at Fryeburg Fair
browses hay from a neat
black canvas bag
and intermittently
stares at me intently
in absolute silence
except for the deliberate
crushing of dried grass
between the teeth.

Its eyes are black
in sockets set deep
below meaningful brows
overhung by straight black hair;
a Hindustani face
in equanimity
contemplating me.

.

What wisdom is this?
Does it differ from
the still, silent
wisdom of a cat?
a sage?
the Buddha?

A woman in attendance
at two stalls of
llamas and alpacas

smiles at them, hugs them
in turn in seeing to their feed
then smiles at me.

I say, "This one
(the one studying me)
is really a beauty."
She smiles in empathy,
"If you love them
 they all are beautiful."

Photograph on the Prairie

Gently undulating fields of shin-high stubble
extend to the horizon, as though the combines
had just now finished their work. Two in the foreground
walk the furrows, absorbed in the moment
which reaches all around them into past and future.

She, at twenty, in a plain cotton dress, loosely tailored
to early pregnancy, her long hair straight and wispy,
looks down as she walks, smiling, her face filled with
happiness gleaned from all the fields around her.
Her long flowing skirt lends its grace to stubble and soil.
Her arms, long and lithe, are strong and ready.
He, at twenty-four, in jeans, short-sleeved plaid shirt,
and shoulder-length hair, looks over and slightly down
at her, smiling with as much joy as a face can hold.

He grips her right hand with strength and tenderness
and the fullness of youthful confidence.
His left arm, darkly tanned to the shirt sleeve,
more muscular than one might expect
in one of his build, balances the empty sleeve
on his right, which, like the missing arm
has no role in their awareness.

Epiphany of a Physicist

The scientist has faith in experimental
procedure. If it fails to reveal the object,
the procedure is modified and carried forward
with equal faith that the object will manifest itself.
The result is not prejudged, but accepted,
as in turning a problem over to That.

In the first half of the twentieth century,
atomic physicists observed results that flew
in the face of established wisdom,
the mathematics of Newton and even of
common sense, but they persevered
in the manner of the Buddha.

By the end of the century, physicists still had
no clear picture of the nature of the atom
and its parts, could not yet fully answer Heisenberg
(mentor late in life of Capra),
who asked himself again and again,
on a lonely walk in '27, after late-night discussions
with Bohr, "Can nature possibly be as absurd
as it seems to us in these experiments?"
Nevertheless, the physicists persevere.

In the late sixties, Fritjof Capra, atomic physicist,
had an epiphany. Sitting on the beach,
absorbed in the rhythms of his breathing and the sea,
he experienced his total immersion

in a great cosmic dance. His work with
mathematical formulae, the birth of new particles
in fireworks-like collisions of subatomic particles
in cloud chambers, his knowledge that showers
of cosmic particles charge into the upper atmosphere
and into his body, colliding with molecules
in cells and air, all of this came vitally alive for him.

It was a revelation beyond any function
of the intellect, and was thus remote
from his many years of work,
a vision of physical realities he had known
only approximately through experiment.
He knew he had realized what Hindu mystics know
as the Dance of Shiva. That infinitely vast reality,
beyond understanding, had been momentarily
manifested in him. The experience
was to define the path to *The Tao of Physics*.

A colleague of mine in the sixties, a chemist, dismissed
out of hand as unworthy Raynor Johnson's plea
in *The Imprisoned Splendor* for scientists to accept
psychic phenomena as a valid field to investigate,
thus violating his unspoken pledge as a scientist
to investigate all phenomena without prejudice.
In this way, generations of scientists have stifled
the unorthodox. Capra, in contrast, aware of the realities
of professional rejection, courageously followed his Heart.

The sixties saw the experimental introduction

by Chuck Cazeau at the State University at Buffalo
of an elective course in psychic phenomena. It had
to be scheduled in the largest lecture room on campus.
The unexpected demand reflected an imprisoned hunger,
a hunger manifested in the eighties and nineties
in the migration of the laity to Hatha Yoga classes
and Buddhist sanghas, followed by consolidation
of parishes and selling off of sanctuaries, as leaders
of church and synagogue tenaciously clung to orthodoxies
more pertinent to the millennia flanking the birth of Jesus.

We are in the midst of a revolution. The answers from my youth
to questions then thought impertinent no longer have validity.
Atheists take the literary stage, adopt the in-your-face
attitudes of current culture, and draw large audiences.
In the midst of this, Capra writes and moves, a quiet voice
of compassion and unquestionable competence,
performing such feats as transforming a book-length treatise
in difficult, convoluted prose by David Bohm into
a page and a half of simple, profound clarity, and moving
small groups of us toward accepting as reality
the absolute interconnectedness of all that is.

Carnegie Hall

I am walking to Carnegie Hall from Penn Station
carrying a boxy briefcase packed with books
and bags of crackers, cheese and peanuts
(a vegetarian, I never get caught short)
after the train ride down from Portland
to hear the Julliard Orchestra and Choral Union,
with my daughter in the Union, perform
Mahler's Resurrection Symphony.

Around the corner from the entrance
construction barriers partly block the way
and a monstrous, open dumpster squats
at the curb, filled to brimming with rubble of rock.
A woman in slacks is picking over the larger cobbles
by streetlight. Curious, I stop to watch. She speaks.
"This stuff is being hauled up from six floors down
below Carnegie Hall. They're expanding something
down there—Imagine! It's the bedrock
under Carnegie Hall. My apartment has a roof garden.
These rocks look great sitting along the walls.
Oh, I wish I were a geologist."

In my twenty-five years as a geologist, nobody
had ever said that to me. I offer to help. The rock
is standard high-rank gneiss, mottled by irregular
crowds of loosely held flakes of clear and black mica.
It has the limited charm of subtle bandedness.
I pick out a couple of representative chunks

for her and a small piece for me (out of habit).
while offering a few semi-technical comments.
I find a niche for my specimen in the briefcase
and walk around to the entrance.

A line leads to a guard, examining things.
It has been only three months since 9/11.
"Man," I think, "He is not going to like this rock."
I step aside, slip the specimen out of the briefcase
and into a pocket and return to the line.
The guard opens the case, looks in, pokes about
and says, "Man, looks like you're gonna have a picnic!"
Freed, I mount the many flights to a seat I can afford.

During the performance, my daughter would have been
barely recognizable, even if my eyes were good
but she is singing at Carnegie Hall; it is enough.
Afterwards we go for coffee. Getting seated,
I pull the specimen from my mica-flake-lined pocket
and am relating my pre-performance experience
when the waitress walks over. "Look," I say,
"This came out of the bedrock under Carnegie Hall."
All the indifference in the world
is enfolded in her utter unresponsiveness
What can I say about this boredom?
What can anyone say? Who needs
rock chunks out of a dumpster?

Back in Maine, I notice a line in the program
touting the gift shop. I carefully cut out

"Carnegie Hall Gift Shop," glue it
to a smooth side of the bit of Carnegie
bedrock, grinning all the while,
and ship it to my daughter.

Euclidian and Other Dreams

Thirty-five years ago, at administrative meetings
I was a doodler with a ballpoint pen.
The doodles, random geometries
some in three dimensions
were filed away as "artwork."

Last year, I mentioned this to my Jungian
analyst, and brought in the doodles file.
He kept it for a week and said, "Sketch."

I began sketching a few minutes a day
in the same old way, random geometries,
using colored pencils to heighten and shade,
a peaceful process, drawing the mind away.

A dream arose of a multitude of people,
clearly discernable but physically together as one;
a small mass of humanity, interpenetrating,
utterly responsive, in a joyful oneness
of loving-kindness. I was with them; an observer.

————————————

Once in a great while,
deep within that which I call *myself*
perfect Euclidian geometries appear
on the screen of my awareness in dream sleep.

The first was a solid yellow cylinder, seated
by bending its middle, and demonstrating

torso-like flexibility with a flair.
Nothing could have been more natural.
The cylinder was self-aware, and, oh, it was vivid.

In a year or so came a still life;
a complex, precisely-rendered rack
of deep blue compressor pipes. Long
straight and looped tubes of small diameter
expanded gracefully into short sections
having three times the girth. To what
was I to relate these exquisite tubes
or the yellow cylinder?

Then, I was in a store. Small, wafer-thin
metal plates were the stock in trade,
brassy gold, rectangular, perfectly machined
and polished, and behaving as might be expected
of each collection of shapes in multiple array.
I could play with them with great wonder
and delight. The entire experience was wondrous.

Today, I have no doubt—
that which is within *myself*
can create in my awareness
what it will, but who decides?
Who provides the expert
mechanical artistry?
What is this *myself?*

_____

The shapes and compressor pipes

represent ultimate loveliness
in physical reality, of which, as yet,
when awake, I have little awareness.
These images do not pass as thoughts, but
remain long enough to be carefully observed.

I have gained a brief experience
of the difference between thoughts
and imagination, a gain
worth many years of seeking.
The beautiful loving people remain,
an embodiment of the goal.

I know of no teacher who points to a way
to transcend the limn between dream sleep
and the waking state. I have no higher
priority than to learn to relate to others
as the dream people relate to themselves
but in all their beauty, they live there
and I here. I have no bridge.

It is late in life. My vision blurs,
even behind corrective lenses.
I can no longer sketch in detail.
The colored pencils, though, are at the ready.
In my mind, step by tenacious step,
I follow a circuitous path
to the dream people's way and beyond.

Girl Child

Prelude
Visiting a relative, a retired missionary,
a born-again Christian, I borrowed
her laptop, and stumbled on a story
posted on her e-mail by a friend,
the story of Danae, which burned itself
deeply into my awareness, and shines through
and beyond my non-theistic acceptance of Brahman,
the ground of all reality, as an unfolding
of the implicate order, an irrefutable
explication of the unbroken wholeness.

———————————————

In Texas, a girl child delivered at twenty-four weeks
by cesarean section, was given a 10 percent chance
to live through the night, or, if she lived, a prognosis
of never walking, never talking, possible blindness
and potentially living with cerebral palsy
or complete mental retardation. The father
was advised to make precautionary arrangements
for a funeral. The mother would not, could not listen.
"No! No! That is not going to happen.
I don't care what the doctors say. Danae
is not going to die. One day she will be just fine.
She will be coming home with us."

All pertinent medical procedures and equipment
were brought to bear. During the first two months,
no one could hold the child. Her skin and nerve endings
were too sensitive for touching. The all-important

early cuddling was not possible. The mother could only
ask God to stay close. Slowly, against all predictions,
the child began to gain. At four months, in the face
of continuing negative prognoses, Danae went home.

———————————————

By her sixth year, Danae was a petite, feisty girl.
with a deep zest for life. None of the predicted mental
or physical impairments had manifested in her body.
On a hot summer afternoon, seated in her mother's lap,
chattering nonstop and watching her brother play ball,
Danae said, "Do you smell that?" An approaching
thunder storm had brought a soft gust of wind.
"Yes," said her mother, "it smells like rain."
"No," said Danae, "it smells like him.
It smells like God when you lay your head
on his chest." Danae jumped down to play.

Her mother's eyes filled with tears, as she realized
in her Heart what she had known unconsciously
in her mind from the beginning of this trial; That
which she knows as God, given unwavering faith
and unconditional love, can substitute for the womb.

Postlude
Danae accepted without condition
that which her mother called out to
many times during her first few months
without affectionate human touch.
The experience will undergird her life.
About that experience the child
has told us all we are likely to learn.

Imagined Inquisition

When Danae was eleven,
a panel of atheists and skeptics
asked permission of her mother
to interrogate the child.

On the strength of her great faith
in the faith of the child
the mother granted an interview
which many would have deemed unwise.

A leader among atheists
towering over the child
put to her one question:
How do you know
it was God's chest
your head was resting on?

Danae responded without hesitation
in deep empathy with That
within her inquisitor,
"In the presence of God,
if you are open to Him,
you know. You do not
need to ask, 'Who are you?'"

Lesson in Patience in April

This morning in the side yard
the wheel of a neighbor's bicycle
that lay under a snowdrift all winter
was released from the ice
and slowly turned in the wind.

J. Sherrard Rice, Churchman

When I was a boy in Virginia
in the largest Southern city
between Atlanta and Baltimore
the south side of the broad main street
had two department stores, each occupying
a city block, patronized by whites alone.
Blacks shopped in smaller stores
on the north side. If a black man
were to have walked along the south side
sidewalk, a white man could have bumped him
into the gutter, without fear of consequences
but such occasions were rare. The larger stores
have been torn down, sacrificed to malls
and their own outlying branches.
Blacks now go where they will
but it's been a long, hard road.

My brother-in-law, a chaplain in World War II,
had graduated from Union Theological Seminary
in Richmond. He earned a ThM at Princeton in '46.
The theme of his thesis, *The Challenge of the Negro
in the Southern Church,* he would have been advised
not to take up at Union. Dr. Rice loved the darky
as did many, but the Negro was expected to stay
in his predetermined place, and to act within
the ill-defined, but thoroughly absorbed
shadow of "the darky," a projection
of the loyalty, jovial friendliness and deep

spirituality of Negroes in the South. The pressure
of the predetermined place infiltrated the land.
To this doctrine, Dr. Rice was loathe to adhere.

After serving congregations in West Virginia and Texas
Dr. Rice was called to First Presbyterian Church, Columbia,
South Carolina, a prestigious position for a young cleric
but a pulpit from which, in 1860, one could have heard
scripture quoted in defense of slavery. The first year
went famously. Most in the congregation were well pleased
with their deeply devout, knowledgeable pastor,
his compassion and unselfishness. They would
soon be introduced to the depths of his courage.

In the late fifties, the challenge of the Negro
had become palpable. Governor Orval Faubus of Arkansas
had strutted across the stage, leaving federalized
National Guard troops escorting black students
to the high school in Little Rock. All across the South
white clerics and deacons dreaded the inevitable Sunday
when a black family would enter the vestibule
and expect to be seated for the service.

On November 30, 1960, J. Sherrard Rice
stepped up to the pulpit in Columbia. He had taken
the precaution of not scheduling a radio broadcast
of the service that Sunday. He wanted to be sure
to say what he was about to say only among friends.
The printed topic of the sermon was
A Pastor Speaks from His Heart. He announced

that he wanted to speak on something that had long
burdened his heart. He would now
take up the topic of his thesis at Princeton.

I hope you will understand that I must speak.
I could not remain your pastor longer unless I did.
In a tense silence, the congregation focused
on the solitary pastor. He recounted two incidents
from his own Southern past, in which individual
Negroes, one well known to him, had been humiliated
in his presence by having to move to the back of a bus.
He told of the agony in his heart when
he kept silent as a witness to these events.

He related anecdotes of Peter and Paul
and their selflessness in answering calls
to preach to the hated Gentiles. He quoted
Genesis 1:27, "God created man in his own image,"
and noted its unavoidable applicability to blacks
and whites alike. *The black man knows it, too.*
That is why, today, he holds his head high
and walks proudly toward the sunrise.

He reminded the congregation of the Great
Commandments, "Thou shalt love the Lord thy God
with all thy heart ... , ... and thy neighbor as thyself."
You know and I know that that means that somehow
we must learn anew, daringly, creatively
what it means to love our neighbor
in our present context, not just as the white man

loves the darky, but as one man made
in the image of God loves another. My conviction
is that we cannot greet change with fear
but as disciples of our Lord Jesus Christ
we must confront it with the outstretched arms of love.

Other Gospel references followed, each familiar
to the congregation, each pertinent in its own way
to *The Challenge of the Negro*; " … preach the Gospel
to every creature." " … a house of prayer for all nations."
"He is our peace, who has broken down
the middle wall of partition between us."
"There is neither bond nor free, neither male nor female,
for ye are all one in Christ Jesus." He ended with,
Let us not be afraid to go where Jesus goes before.
Then he prayed. *Help us to respect one another. Help us*
to be able to look at things differently, and yet always
together as Christians. Take possession of our Southland;
take possession of our country. May the Spirit enable us
to shake off the bondage of fear and move forward into
a new day, into the glorious liberty of all sons of God.

He had opened the door just enough
to let in a thin shaft of light that was to him,
and he knew would be to almost all of them,
unassailable, thus deftly transforming
a potential conflict between a pastor
and his congregation into a matter between
the white Christian and his God.
There would be no turning back.

Intelligent Design

Waiting in the workout room for the physical therapist,
intrigued by anatomical charts, artists' impressions
of patterns of muscles and tendons in arms, legs and torsos,
I realized, these represent intelligent design,
and grinned to myself, "I'm a believer."
Accepter would be better, for one
who accepts truth as it unfolds.

The charts depict only cadaverous impressions,
not the truth of life, which could be approached
only by observing these muscles flushed with blood
au natural, and functioning in response to the nerves.
Even so, the exquisite artistry and complexity
of the utilitarian design and the potential
for multiple interactions are deeply impressive.

Having all this manifest itself as a cohesive whole
without the guidance of an external reality
may be hard to imagine, but then,
we scarcely can even imagine
the time available for the process,
which began with our single-celled
cousins in residence, who gave rise
to all these forms in becoming our bodies,
the flayed cadavers on the wall.

As I mused, the therapist approached.
I smiled, indicating the charts, and said,

"This is intelligent design." He was nonplussed,
despite the recent arguments in the media
contrasting evolution and design, but no matter,
the body seems intelligently designed
(with only a slip up here and there), by the designer-
model-maker-manufacturer of soft-bodied creatures,
who employs only single-celled crews.

William James, though, points us to a seeming
elsewhere, the subliminal stream of ideal tendency,
embedded in space in all dimensions,
infinitely manifesting and unmanifesting
as braided streams of joyful sorrow;
the eternal subtle structure of the universe;
not a model maker, but the all-encompassing All.

Our task is not to choose, but to accept each
as necessary aspects of all that is
like sub-atomic particles and their waves
between which physicists cannot choose.

What I Might Have Said to Doug
at His Farewell Party on the Lawn

As guests began to leave, I leaned against the casing
of the open overhead door, tables of partly-eaten desserts
at my back, caterer's people and others still cleaning up,
Doug on my right adjusting his touch-controlled wheelchair-
lounge chair on occasion, using the few muscles still
functioning in his right arm. Both legs and the left arm
had been gone since last year, but his smile was fully intact.

It was a great family gathering, with kids knocking a soccer ball about
behind the picnic tables. Dozens of the hundred guests
still mingled about, family, friends, coworkers, many of whom
doubled as associates on the spiritual way, Quakers, Buddhists,
Christians, none laboring under any false hope that ALS
might spare this man in the motorized chair.

Earlier, while memories were being recounted, eulogies
in the midst of life, I watched Doug closely. He drank it all in.
The smile from the depths of his soul never left his face.
Every one who spoke, and there were many, some at length,
was someone who loved him, whom he loved; Such a harvest!
—a pouring out of all that had been gathered in.

Doug spoke earnestly, humorously, with each of us
who came up to share one more thought with him on this day
tenaciously set aside by Doug and Joan. My thought was,
You are our teacher, even more strongly now than during
all the years from childhood on, our exemplar

of courage and joy in the face of impossible odds.

After a few weeks, Doug took his leave. Not being among
the closer circle of family and friends, the party
was my last sight of him, but his memory and message
remain within me—a great gathering of the joyful
sorrow that passes all understanding.

Luna

The death in the lunar surface belies the serenity of the light
reflected from its chaos of rock chunks and powder,
pummeled about incessantly through endless time,
one crater at a time, buried by lava, cooled,
re-excavated by catastrophic cosmic encounter,
quiescent for ten thousand millennia, jostled again.

The rock, anhydrous, has no water-bearing minerals;
even the friendly mica is missing. The surface material
has no moisture, not even a molecule, but intolerable heat
and unendurable cold, the antithesis of the romantic
ambiance we transfer to Earth in the moon's reflection.

This is the romance of the universe, endless process,
one reality giving way to another; no provision for life, except
here and there, where conditions are just so, infinitesimal
incidents in the patterns, integral aspects of the ongoing,
intellectually ungraspable mystery we are well advised
to accept as it is, at the level of the gut or Heart, while,
as need be, stepping out of the way of the process
for self-preservation, or standing as a shield for another
like a soft hydrated rock, offering itself without fear, question
or reservation, to help one or the many one has learned to love.

God Is

"Something there is that doesn't
love a wall," does not refer to God.
Piling up against acceleration
and the activity of creatures and plants
will not be tolerated long.

God is not something,
not anything. Things perish.
There is no truth in "God is not,"
but "There is nothing" has truth,
is not in conflict with the Presence.

God is the presence inherent
in the universe by virtue of its nature,
"the imbedded stream of ideal tendency"
to which the intellect cannot add,
from which it cannot take away.

All is relationship, in movement.
God is that which replies, guides, leads,
the always ever ongoing accessible
Presence; our deepest nature.

Cards and Other Games

A Virginian, late in life I married a Nova Scotian,
one of a large clan given to card games
at any suggestion, in any gathering of three.
In Liverpool Rummy, one competes
with one's own fortune in drawing cards.
Given decent skill in keeping it organized
and a touch of serendipity, your score
(or lack of it) can increase almost in spite
of yourself. This game is benign—
it fills an evening well, but for those desiring
a bit of a bite in the proceedings, we have
Forty-Fives, the national card game
of Nova Scotia. Partners compete
in cleverness in bidding, in the attempt
to pile up score. Serendipity occupies
a lesser place. For those learning to compete,
mostly male grandchildren in their teens
and twenties, this game is an object lesson
in forging ahead over the fortunes of others.

Other family members subtly or overtly
cheer them on, so that one learns competition
by approval and the example of its effectiveness.
The expressions of anticipation on the faces
of several males, young and old, on approaching
the table are markedly and delightedly predatory.
The family has a lot of fun with this game.

Last summer I sat at Forty-Fives, opposite
a young male partner who managed to temper
with kindness his exasperation at my poor playing.
Experienced players tend to help me, but how long
can I string along the beginner's game?
My wife has often offered lessons
but I decline. She understands, knows
I desire to live a life of completion,
not competition; not to gain, but to give.
In that game of life, vigilance is key.
Being drawn in to Forty-Fives reinforces
the competitive edge our society
overtly and subliminally sharpens.

Last time, then, at Thanksgiving I stood aside,
caught a few running and passing plays
on the telly, and let the card games roll.
I felt a little lonely, but uncompromised
and silently worked on the mantrum,
which extinguishes the illusion of boredom.
I don't mind the loss of an afternoon's entertainment.
Sometimes, I have to remind myself
to let an afternoon go. My wife, though,
my first reader, did not like this stanza.

Bringers of New Things

Some run up hill and down dale
whacking the stones to pieces with hammers;
analyzing optically-thin slices and kilogram chunks;
studying mountains with the microscope and crucible.
They say it is to see how the world was made.

Some endlessly pipette into rack after rack
of test tubes, to track the movement of molecules
from cell to cell in the brain and autonomic
nervous system, to map the neurobiochemistry
of disease and pin down the ground of emotion.

A few accelerate particles on the subatomic scale
causing collisions, to analyze the arcuate, fireworks-like
bursts of new particles in a magnetic field
in the search for an ultimate pattern,
a force uniting all reality. A few
scan the night sky, by use of telescopes
of unprecedented range and resolution
to seek the beginning on the macro scale
of that which has not been shown to have an end.

Most walk ordinary paths in no extraordinary way.
They have little contact with those who whack,
pipette, accelerate or scan, but are in no way at all
apart from them, unless they feel so in their minds.
They seek the resolution of their lives
and have as much grasp of their own identity

as those who accelerate particles,
the margins of whose untraveled worlds
fade forever and forever as they probe,
bringing something more, endless showers
of particles, beyond understanding
but within the boundless realm of realization.

Such are our bringers of new things, toward whom
Ulysses leans, feeling right at home, while Krishna
dispassionately looks on, seeing nothing new
and waits with infinite patience for the dawn.

August Morning

My breakfast window
opens to the sun.
Cool damp air
pours over the table
into my lap.

Behind a rim of trees
the misty cove
has been subsumed
in white brilliance.

Begin the day.
Embrace the East.
Let go.
Abandon yourself
to brilliance.

Credits

Publication Credit. H. D. is grateful to the editors of the following magazine for publishing the poem listed.

Reflections, "Homo *Faber*"

Notes, Definitions

Augustine and Einstein. Both were aware of the relativity of time. See Augustine, *Confessions,* Book Eleven.

American Legacy. The image of the terrified girl is an Associated Press photograph that appeared in the Portland, Maine, *Press Herald* on July 9, 2004. Part II was inspired by an article in *Newsweek* entitled, *Orphans of Tall Afar,* by Owen Matthews, with photographs by Chris Hondros, in the issue of March 28, 2005, p. 34-35.

Coevolutionary. Having existed and evolved inseparably.

Epiphany of a Physicist. For the summary of David Bohm's, *Wholeness and The Implicate Order,* see Fritjof Capra, *The Tao of Physics*, Second Edition, p. 319-320.

Girl Child was inspired by the story, *Heaven Scent,* in the book, *Miracles in our Midst,* by Richard L. Scott.

Gleanings. Father Edward J. McLean has kindly given permission to include the partial passage quoted in this poem, which was taken from an oral presentation in his ongoing CD series, *Journey from the Head to the Heart.*

God Is. "Something there is that doesn't love a wall" is the first line of Robert Frost's poem, *Mending Wall.* "All is relationship, in movement" reflects ideas of Fritjof Capra and David Bohm.

Heart, when capitalized, implies the non-biological heart, the seat of the Self (in the Hindu sense). When not capitalized, heart refers to the blood pump and the white blood cells, following the usage of Candace Pert in *Molecules of Emotion*, and may, therefore, refer to the brain.as well.

Heather Marie, at Sixteen, was largely inspired by an article in *Church World* by Thomas J. Kardos on March 22, 2001, that included testimony from Heather's parents, her pastor, her maternal grandmother, the organist at the church where Heather is cantor, and many others. *Church World* is published by the Roman Catholic Bishop of Portland, Maine.

Homo *Faber,* man the builder, the user of tools, as opposed to Homo *sapiens,* man the wise one or thinker.

Implicate order. A term proposed by David Bohm for the mutual infolding (as in plication) of all reality; the order implied in the universe through and beyond the application of quantum theory. See also, *interpenetration.*

Interpenetration includes the principle of "all in each and each in all." Fritjof Capra says, in *The Tao of Physics,* p. 293, "The experience of interpenetration in the state of enlightenment can be seen as mystical visions" *in which,* " ... all phenomena in the universe are harmoniously interrelated. In such a state of consciousness, the intellect is transcended and causal explanations become unnecessary, being replaced by the direct experience of the mutual interdependence of all things and events."

J. Sherrard Rice, Churchman. Dr. Rice's words (in italics) and the scriptural quotes have been taken from a transcript of his November 30, 1960 sermon in an autobiography by Molly Wagener Rice, *Molly's Book,* by permission of the author. The impression of the congregation near the beginning of stanza six is from recent commentary by an attendee at the service, Sherrard's son Hunter, who was twelve at the time.

Limn. A boundary between the unreal and the real, or between the conscious and unconscious; a curtain drawn by the mind, whose surface may be occasionally observed internally.

March 20, 2004. *when Earth resumes its old subtropical nature.* For the last eight hundred million years or so, the climate of Earth has been substantially warmer than it is now. We live in (or on the fringe of) one of only three known, very short periods of cold weather, in which large parts of the surface have been covered with ice.

Morning Event. The last two lines in this poem are a refutation of H. D.'s approach to life prior to age sixty.

Photograph on the Prairie. The photograph described, by Ethan Hubbard, is entitled, *Prairie Sweethearts.* It appeared inside the back cover of *The Sun* June 2007 issue.

Rule: Ahimsa Paramo Dharma. *Ahimsa is the highest law.* Ahimsa (non-injury) may be thought of as "nonviolence," but this is a pale approximation of its full nature.

"When all violence has subsided in my heart, my native state is love … even avoiding a person we dislike can be a subtle form of *himsa* (injury) or violence. Therefore, in everyday terms, ahimsa often means bearing with difficult people."—*Eknath Easwaran*

"Ahimsa is an attribute of the soul and therefore is to be practiced by everybody in all affairs of life." —*Gandhi*

"Nonviolence (ahimsa) is seated in the Heart and must be an integral part of one's being. It implies complete self-purification." —*Gandhi.*

Gandhi referred to the Bhagavad Gita as his mother. He considered the Gita and the Sermon on the Mount to be the same teaching; therefore, H. D. has attempted a partial integration (lines 26 to 55). Essentially, lines 10 through 55 comprise an interfaith Golden Rule.

Sources: Lines 1–9, teachings of Mohandas K. Gandhi in early twentieth-century pamphlets (www.gandhiserve.org). Lines 10 and 11, 14–23, 26 and 27, the Bhagavad Gita (The Song of the Lord), translation by Eknath Easwaran. Lines 26–55 contain selected phrases from the Sermon on the Mount, partly paraphrased, and embellished by teachings from Sri Easwaran's translation of the Gita. Also included are thoughts from: George Fox, lines 12 and 13; Siddhartha Gautama, line 17; Vivekananda, line 19; Saul of Tarsus, lines 23 and 24 (in part); *The Cloud of Unknowing*, line 25 (in part).

Ramana Maharshi, a twentieth-century Hindu sage, says that all of Vedanta (the vast storehouse of Hindu scripture, including the Bhagavad Gita) is contained in two short sentences in the Bible: *I am that I am* (*I will be that I will be*), and *Be still and know that I am God.*

Ruth Farabee Clark was inspired by an article entitled "A Life Fully Lived" by Bob Keyes in the *Maine Sunday Telegram*, January 30, 2005, p. E1-E2.

That Which Is. The last four lines of stanza 1 are quoted from, Eknath Easwaran, *The Bhagavad Gita for Daily Living*, V. 2, p. 421.

Timmy Thompson was inspired by two comprehensive investigative reports by Barbara Walsh in the *Maine Sunday Telegram*, November 14, 2004, with family and staff photographs; letters to the editor in the *Maine Sunday Telegram*, November 21, 2000; and a follow-up article by Barbara Walsh in the *Maine Sunday Telegram* in September 2005.

Unbroken wholeness is used here in the sense of, "All is one," or, "Each in all and all in each."

Valentine Shoppers. *Complimentarity*; reflecting each other; a natural similarity in appearance and mannerisms.